This Is Your Government™

THE DEPARTMENT OF ENERGY

Phillip Margulies

rosen
central™

The Rosen Publishing Group, Inc., New York

Published in 2006 by The Rosen Publishing Group, Inc.
29 East 21st Street, New York, NY 10010

Library of Congress Cataloging-in-Publication Data

Margulies, Phillip, 1952–
The Department of Energy / by Phillip Margulies.—1st ed.
    v. cm.—(This is your government)
Includes bibliographical references and index.
Contents: The history of the Department of Energy—The Secretaries of
Energy—How the Department of Energy works—The Department of Energy
in the twenty-first century—Timeline.
ISBN 1-4042-0208-0 (lib. bdg.)
ISBN 1-4042-0661-2 (pbk. bdg.)
1. United States. Dept. of Energy—Juvenile literature. 2. Energy policy—
United States—Juvenile literature. [1. United States. Dept. of Energy.
2. Energy policy.]
I. Title. II. Series.
HD9502.U52M374 2005
333.79'0973—dc22

                                                    2003027581

Manufactured in the United States of America

On the cover: From left to right: James R. Schlesinger, James D. Watkins,
Hazel R. O'Leary, Bill Richardson, Samuel W. Bodman.

CONTENTS

Introduction 5

CHAPTER ONE — The History of the Department of Energy 11

CHAPTER TWO — The Secretaries of Energy 22

CHAPTER THREE — How the Department of Energy Works 35

CHAPTER FOUR — The Department of Energy in the Twenty-first Century 42

Conclusion 53

Timeline 55

Glossary 59

For More Information 60

For Further Reading 61

Bibliography 62

Index 63

Introduction

Americans living in the early years of the twenty-first century have come to rely upon complex technology to help perform the most basic tasks of everyday life. Many of our simple daily tasks and activities are done with the help of machinery, from washing dishes and communicating with each other to preparing meals and traveling to and from school or work. We also use machines for more dramatic and unusual purposes, such as gathering satellite-based information and waging modern war.

We have come to depend on our machines. That means that we have come to rely on a large and constant supply of energy, because machines need energy to run. Whether the source is coal, oil, natural gas, wind, water, nuclear power, or the

Department of Energy Organization Chart

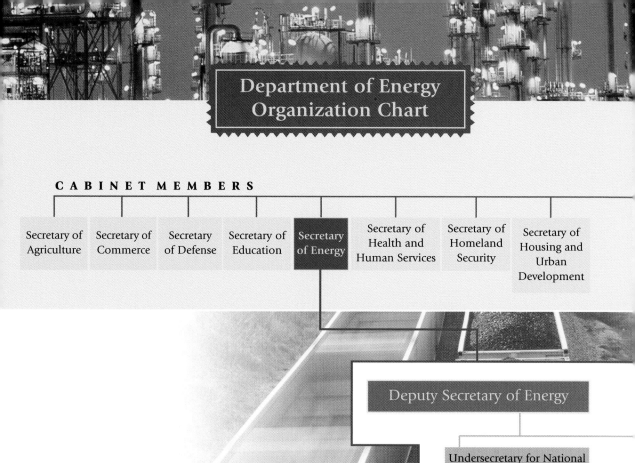

CABINET MEMBERS

| Secretary of Agriculture | Secretary of Commerce | Secretary of Defense | Secretary of Education | Secretary of Energy | Secretary of Health and Human Services | Secretary of Homeland Security | Secretary of Housing and Urban Development |

Deputy Secretary of Energy

Undersecretary for National Nuclear Security/ Administrator for National Nuclear Security Administration

| Deputy Administrator for Defense Programs | Deputy Administrator for Defense Nuclear Nonproliferation | Deputy Administrator for Naval Reactors |

| Emergency Operations | Associate Administrator for Infrastructure and Security | Associate Administrator for Management and Administration |

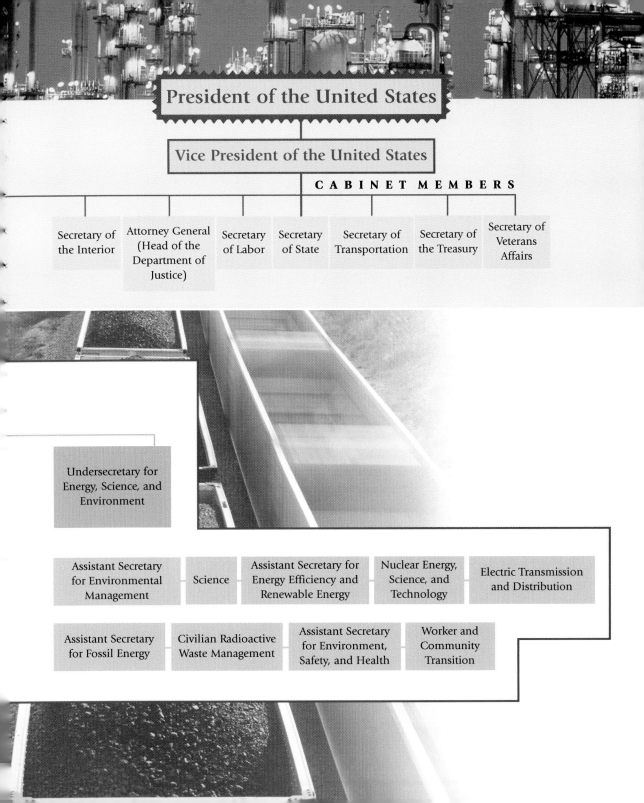

President of the United States

Vice President of the United States

CABINET MEMBERS

Secretary of the Interior	Attorney General (Head of the Department of Justice)	Secretary of Labor	Secretary of State	Secretary of Transportation	Secretary of the Treasury	Secretary of Veterans Affairs

Undersecretary for Energy, Science, and Environment

Assistant Secretary for Environmental Management	Science	Assistant Secretary for Energy Efficiency and Renewable Energy	Nuclear Energy, Science, and Technology	Electric Transmission and Distribution

Assistant Secretary for Fossil Energy	Civilian Radioactive Waste Management	Assistant Secretary for Environment, Safety, and Health	Worker and Community Transition

light of the sun, there must be energy for our society to function. Without energy, the machines stop, as surely as an electric toaster stops when somebody pulls its plug. Computer screens go dark. Telephones become useless hunks of plastic. Airplanes cannot leave the gate. Mills do not make steel. Trucks stop bringing food to towns and cities. Clean tap water does not come out of the faucet. Disrupting the supply of energy to our communities is like stopping the heart in the human body. Our high-tech civilization lives on energy and can quickly become paralyzed without it.

Even small reductions in our energy supply can have huge consequences. The great economic engine of American prosperity slows down, millions of people lose their jobs, and prices rise. We know this because it happened during a gas crisis in the 1970s, the decade in which the Department of Energy (DOE) was founded.

It is the job of the Department of Energy to see to it that the country obtains the energy it needs at a cost Americans can afford. Since energy and energy policy are so vital to the prosperity and security of the United States, the Department of Energy is a cabinet-level department. This means that the person in charge of the department—the secretary of energy—is one of the president's key advisers. The president appoints the secretary of energy with the advice and consent of Congress—that is, a majority of senators and representatives must vote in

At left is an offshore oil rig. It operates like any other oil rig except that it is anchored to the ocean floor where it pumps oil from beneath the earth's surface up to waiting tankers. The photovoltaic devices at right, more commonly known as solar cells, turn sunlight into electricity. Solar cells can provide electricity for satellites, highway traffic signs, telephones, and streetlights.

favor of the appointment. As the head of a department with an annual budget of $25 billion, the secretary of energy possesses an enormous amount of political power and influence.

Energy policy is a complicated business, because energy comes from many sources. Each energy source has its advantages and disadvantages. Energy is also very big business. Each piece of legislation relating to energy policy can represent billions of dollars of profit to some energy companies. Every decision the government makes about energy gladdens the hearts of some citizens and infuriates others. For this reason many of the decisions the Department of Energy makes are intensely controversial, raising numerous difficult questions. Should the DOE put most of its efforts into encouraging conservation (using less energy) or into finding new sources of energy that will allow us to maintain or increase our energy usage? What can be done to reduce America's dependence on foreign oil? Should we let American oil companies drill in Alaska's Arctic National Wildlife Refuge or would such activity be too damaging to that unique and delicate environment? Should the Department of Energy discourage the use of fossil fuels (coal and oil), the burning of which poses a threat to humans and their environment? Does nuclear power pose a greater or lesser threat than do fossil fuels? Will alternative and clean energy sources—wind, water, the sun—ever be able to provide the United States with enough power at a low enough price to meet its energy needs? The answers to these and other questions can make a tremendous difference in all of our lives. These are the questions that the secretary of energy must try to answer.

CHAPTER ONE

The History of the Department of Energy

The position of secretary of energy was created by President Jimmy Carter in 1977, during a time when energy policy had come to be considered an extremely urgent matter for the United States. Because of a reduction in output of Middle Eastern oil, people were paying more than ever to fill their gas tanks and heat their houses. The high price of energy—in the form of gasoline, heating oil, and electricity—had pushed up the prices of other goods that were manufactured with the help of energy. High energy costs were bad for businesses, so businesses hired fewer people. Between high prices and high unemployment rates—due in part to the energy crisis—Americans had a lot to complain

A well in Richland, Texas, strikes oil in 1922. Gushers like this are created when oil that is lying under millions of tons of rock is suddenly released by an oil well's drill. The pressure of the rocks' weight and the earth's heat is also released, causing a spurting of oil several hundreds of feet high. Modern oil wells are now equipped with "blowout preventers" that stop these gushers.

about in the 1970s, though the situation was by no means a new one.

America's Increasing Energy Needs

To understand how the energy crisis of the 1970s came about and led directly to the creation of the DOE, it helps to look at the history of energy in the United States. At the time of the country's founding—before the Industrial Revolution and the beginning of the machine age—energy needs were low, and energy was plentiful and locally available. Americans heated their homes with firewood. For light after dark, they used candles and oil-burning lamps. Horses provided transportation. Waterpower from the flow of streams and rivers helped to grind grain into flour and run the machines of the first textile factories. The young country possessed these traditional energy sources in abundance. When mechanized industries—with their enormous energy requirements—began to grow in the United States, new energy sources such as coal and oil had to be tapped. Luckily, America was well supplied with these fossil fuels.

At the beginning of the twentieth century, the first automobiles were introduced. They ran on gasoline derived from oil. America quickly became a nation of motorists, and oil replaced coal as the most important fuel source for both transportation and industry.

During the first half of the twentieth century, oil was plentiful and inexpensive. Global oil prices were so low that American oil companies became worried about losing business to competitors from overseas. As oil fields were discovered and developed in the Middle East, American oil companies asked the U.S. Congress to protect them from Middle Eastern competition and keep prices from dropping too low by taxing imported oil. Congress often agreed to the oil companies' requests.

The Development of Nuclear Power

Nuclear energy was first developed for use in weapons rather than as a source of energy. At the beginning of World War II (1939–1945), U.S. scientists warned President Franklin D. Roosevelt that recent discoveries in physics had made it possible to create a type of bomb so powerful that just one could destroy an entire city. The bomb's power came from unleashing the force that holds the

In the summer of 1946, the U.S. Navy and Air Force conducted joint atom bomb tests near the Bikini Atoll in the South Pacific Ocean to measure the effect of an atomic explosion on ships and unmanned drone aircraft. At left is a mushroom cloud formed after one of these detonations, which destroyed or heavily damaged empty target ships anchored within a half mile (0.8 km) of the blast.

nuclei (the central mass) of atoms together. The energy released by breaking apart these atoms is known as nuclear energy.

As terrifying as the destructive force of the atomic bomb was, many people welcomed the advent of the nuclear age with optimism. It was argued that nuclear power could supply the nation with a limitless source of cheap energy. Every day, people lived with the dread that the United States and the Soviet Union would destroy each other and the entire world in a nuclear war. However, they also lived with the dream that nuclear energy would bring worldwide prosperity by providing abundant energy at very low prices.

In 1947, Congress created the Atomic Energy Commission (AEC) to regulate both the dread and the dream of nuclear power. The AEC controlled the new arsenal of nuclear weapons the United States was creating in its arms race with the Soviet Union. At the same time, it encouraged the development of the nuclear power industry.

In the years that followed the creation of the AEC, safe nuclear power turned out to be a lot more difficult to develop than it had at first appeared. Throughout the 1950s and the 1960s, the promised golden age of unlimited power remained out of reach. In fact, development and generation of nuclear power was so expensive that it could not exist without subsidies (payments) from the government.

The Calm Before the Storm

Throughout the twentieth century, as Americans came to rely more and more on cars and America's farms and factories became increasingly mechanized, America's consumption of energy grew rapidly. By the 1960s, the United States was using more energy than any other country in the world and far more than it could produce. Very few people worried about this growing dependence on foreign energy sources, however. America was rich enough to buy all the extra energy it needed from other countries, especially the countries of the Middle East, where oil was the primary natural resource.

At this time, most Americans did not think much about the nation's energy needs and supply. A handful of experts were beginning to worry, however. If America's demand for energy kept growing, there would be shortages in the future. In 1971 and again in 1973, President Richard M. Nixon addressed Congress, speaking of the need for a new energy policy. Nixon suggested that a cabinet-level department of energy be created.

Most Americans did not agree with him. Energy in the form of foreign oil was still cheap and easily available. By this time, America, only 6 percent of the world's population, was using one-third of the world's yearly energy production.

The 1973 Arab Oil Embargo

The average U.S. citizen's ideas about energy began to change in October 1973, with the beginning of the Arab oil embargo. The biggest oil producers in the world, mostly Arabic-speaking countries in the Middle East, had become organized in two international cartels (groups of producers that have a monopoly or near-monopoly on what they make). The first was called OPEC (the Organization of Petroleum Exporting Countries), which included non-Arab countries such as Iran and Venezuela. The second cartel was a smaller, all-Arab group within OPEC called OAPEC (the Organization of Arab Petroleum Exporting Countries). Having no competition, a cartel can set whatever prices it wants on its product, without having to worry about competitors setting lower prices. The member countries of OAPEC and OPEC produced so much of the world's oil that they could do just that. By agreeing among themselves on how much oil they would pump from their wells at a given time, they could raise or lower the average price of crude oil at will.

OPEC had been formed in 1960 and OAPEC in 1968, but neither group's members had ever been able to agree to limit

OPEC includes eleven developing nations whose economies depend upon the money raised by oil sales to other countries. Representatives of OPEC meet regularly to agree upon the amount of oil they will produce and how much they will charge for it. In this photograph, OPEC oil ministers gather for a meeting in Doha, Qatar, in the mid-1970s.

production of oil, so supplies remained high and prices low. The event that finally unified the cartels was the victory of Israel over Syria and Egypt in the October 1973 Yom Kippur War. Though the United States did not actively participate in that war, it supplied Israel with weapons and money. OAPEC decided to punish the United States for its support of Israel by refusing to ship crude oil to the United States. This became known as the Arab oil embargo.

The embargo did not eliminate America's access to oil. America still produced much of its own oil, and not all

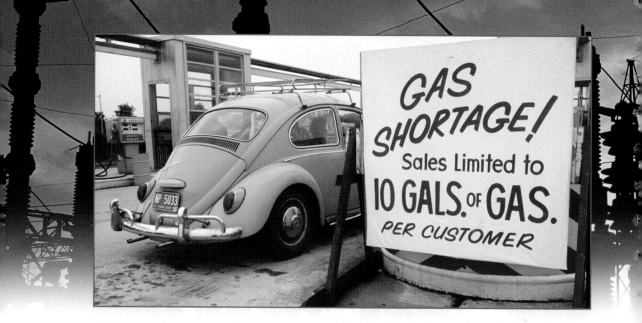

A Connecticut gas station announces that fuel is being rationed during the energy crisis of 1974. The gas shortage was brought about by OPEC's decision to cut oil production and raise prices. As a result, gas was rationed, lines at gas stations stretched for a mile (1.6 km) or more, and station owners often closed by the early afternoon after having sold their daily quota.

petroleum-exporting countries took part in the embargo. But the Arab oil embargo did create shortages and raise the price of energy. The most visible signs of the shortage were around-the-block lines at gas stations all over the country and very high prices for heating oil. In a televised speech on November 7, 1973, soon after the beginning of the embargo, President Nixon launched a program called Project Independence, which set the goal of achieving energy self-sufficiency in the United States by 1980. If the United States reached a point at which it no longer needed to import fuel from abroad, the country could not be held hostage to oil-exporting countries that wanted to influence its foreign policy, as OAPEC was trying to do.

The immediate shortages caused by the Arab oil embargo led more Americans finally to begin thinking about the long-term energy problems facing the country.

The Crisis Eases but Questions Remain

When the Arab oil embargo ended in March 1974, the gas lines disappeared and so, at first, did the feeling that there was an energy "crisis." Oil prices remained high, however. Through the actions of OAPEC members, OPEC, the larger cartel, became aware of its strength. OPEC members realized that even if they could not use their near-monopoly on oil to affect U.S. foreign policy, they could work together to get a better price for each barrel of oil they sold. Thanks to OPEC's oil production cuts, gas prices remained high all over the world long after the embargo ended. Americans and Europeans began to buy the small, fuel-efficient cars the Japanese were producing, which used much less gas per mile than larger American cars did.

The presidential administrations of Gerald Ford (1974–1977) and Jimmy Carter (1977–1981) continued to try to develop a national energy policy. Plans were made to explore new oil reserves in Alaska and to develop nuclear energy further in the United States. Americans began to debate the solutions to the energy problem. Should gasoline be taxed to encourage people to conserve energy? Should nuclear power be developed

THE DEPARTMENT OF PETROLEUM AT WORK: THE STRATEGIC PETROLEUM RESERVE

For more than fifty years, many American politicians and Energy Department officials have recognized the importance of setting aside a supply of fuel in the United States in case of emergency shortages of foreign oil. The 1973 to 1974 oil embargo finally made the government commit to an oil reserve. In the aftermath of the energy crisis, the United States established the Strategic Petroleum Reserve. President Gerald Ford created the SPR when he signed the Energy Policy and Conservation Act on December 22, 1975. From then on, oil owned by the federal government would be stored in huge underground salt caverns along the coastline of the Gulf of Mexico. These caverns have the capacity to hold 700 million barrels of oil. The SPR is the largest emergency petroleum stockpile in the world.

despite its dangers? Should alternative energy sources, such as solar power, be explored?

Seeking Solutions

Even as Americans became aware of the problems caused by high energy prices, more and more people were also concerned about the environmental problems caused by the most commonly used energy sources. Coal mining damaged the landscape. Burning coal and oil added to air pollution. Nuclear power created dangerous radioactive waste products and the potential for disastrous nuclear accidents. Regulations that would make energy production less harmful to the environment would drive up the cost of energy. Americans wanted a healthy environment, but they also wanted cheap energy. How could both of these desires be met?

While successfully campaigning against President Gerald Ford in 1976, Jimmy Carter promised to create a cabinet-level Department of Energy to address these questions and seek solutions. Soon after his inauguration, Carter appointed James R. Schlesinger to study the energy problem and present a comprehensive plan to Congress. On February 2, 1977, Carter addressed the nation in a fireside chat, stressing the need for conservation to solve the energy problem. In April, sending his energy legislation to Congress, Carter described the energy crisis as "the moral equivalent to war." On August 4, 1977, Carter signed the bill that created the Department of Energy. The Department of Energy officially became active on October 1, 1977, with Schlesinger as its first secretary.

CHAPTER TWO

The Secretaries of Energy

The Department of Energy is one of the newer cabinet offices, having been created in 1977. Between the time of its birth and the time of the writing of this book in 2004, the DOE has existed through five presidential administrations and has been headed by ten secretaries.

Secretaries of energy, like all cabinet members, work to carry out the wishes of the president who appointed them. The policies of the various secretaries of energy have always tended to reflect the aims of the president in office at the time. These aims have varied greatly, depending on which party the president belonged to, as well as on the country's changing energy needs.

James R. Schlesinger

James R. Schlesinger was the first and most influential secretary of energy. Under President Jimmy Carter, Schlesinger helped to draft the law that created the DOE and formulated the country's basic strategies for dealing with the energy crisis of the 1970s.

Though he was appointed by Carter, a Democrat, James Schlesinger was a Republican. Before he became secretary of the Energy Department, he had at different times been chairman of the Atomic Energy Commission, director of the Central Intelligence Agency (the CIA; America's spy network), and secretary of the Defense Department. Carter relied on Schlesinger to help him create his energy plan and design the DOE. Schlesinger even helped write the proposals outlining the DOE's responsibilities that would be sent to Congress for approval.

Carter and Schlesinger put together a large and detailed energy program. The five major energy acts that were signed into law made a stack of paper nine inches (twenty-three centimeters) high. At the time, the price of domestically produced oil—oil produced in the United States—was controlled by the government so that it was lower than the price for oil produced elsewhere in the world. This was meant to encourage the use of American oil and to reduce dependence on foreign sources. Schlesinger, however, wanted to deregulate domestic oil prices. This means that he wanted to remove government control over them and let them rise to the level of the prices charged overseas.

To encourage conservation of oil, Schlesinger wanted to place a tax on it. Very few Americans wanted to pay more for gasoline, even if it was supposed to be good for the economy and the environment. Sensing the voters' disapproval, Congress rejected the deregulation and tax portions of the Carter administration's energy plan. Carter said his original proposals would have lowered oil imports by an estimated 4.5 million barrels per day by 1985. In its final form, the new legislation would reduce imports by 2.5 million barrels per day.

Aside from Carter's controversial and sweeping energy policy, two other incidents occurred while Schlesinger was in office that had long-term effects on American energy policy and the work of the secretary of energy—the Iranian revolution and the crisis at the Three Mile Island nuclear power plant.

A New Energy Shortage

On January 16, 1979, there was a revolution in Iran, a major oil-exporting country. The country's former leader, Shah Mohammad Reza Pahlavi, an American ally, was forced to flee the country. Iran was in the throes of the twentieth century's first fundamentalist Islamic revolution—a takeover of the country by a group of Muslims committed to setting up a strict religious government. The new Iranian regime stopped exporting oil and soon created a worldwide shortage. Other oil-exporting nations took advantage of the situation and raised their prices.

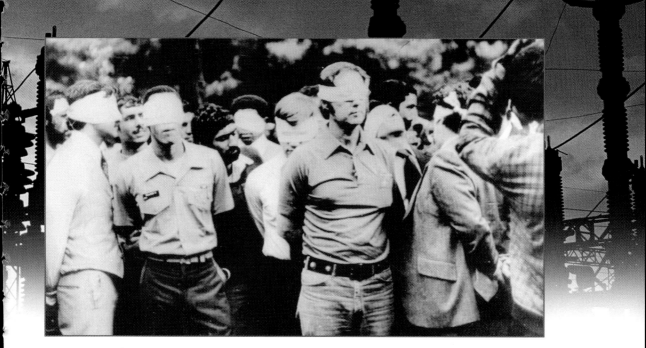

On November 4, 1979, as many as 3,000 followers of Iran's new Islamic fundamentalist leader, Ayatollah Ruholla Khomeini, seized control of the American Embassy in Tehran and took sixty-six Americans hostage. This photo was taken on the first day of their captivity. Most of the hostages were held for 444 days before finally being released.

Carter called on the United States to conserve energy voluntarily until normal oil supplies were again available. The United States was in the midst of a new energy crisis.

Once again there were lines around the block to fill tanks at gas stations, and fuel prices were skyrocketing. In order to control fuel use and reduce the gas lines, drivers were only allowed to buy gas on alternate days. Their fill-up days were assigned based on whether their license plates ended with an odd or even number. President Carter delivered a speech on the crisis and his energy policy. He said that there was no single answer to the nation's energy woes. He outlined a very detailed and complex policy that combined more energy production, more conservation, and the use of subsidies to help develop alternative energy sources. Together, these proposals were meant to cut energy use and reduce dependence on foreign suppliers.

The Three Mile Island Accident

On March 28, 1979, in the midst of the energy crisis, the United States experienced a major nuclear accident. In the early hours of that Wednesday morning, two water pumps in the cooling system at Three Mile Island, a large nuclear power plant in the small town of Harrisburg, Pennsylvania, simply stopped operating. A series of errors in the automated operating system of the plant and on the part of plant staff quickly resulted in the worst nuclear accident in U.S. history.

Had the situation not been brought under control in time, it might have led to the worst of all possible human-made disasters: total nuclear meltdown. Thankfully, no one was killed or even injured as a result of the Three Mile Island disaster. It did leave the power plant inoperable, however, and cost nearly $1 billion to clean up. More important, it had a serious and lasting effect on American nuclear energy policy and development.

The disaster at the plant changed the way the public viewed nuclear energy. People became far more skeptical of the limitless and "safe" uses of nuclear fuel. Not a single new nuclear power plant has been ordered in the United States

On March 28, 1979, a malfunctioning valve at the Three Mile Island nuclear power plant badly damaged the plant's Unit-2 reactor and almost resulted in a disastrous meltdown of its nuclear core. This photograph shows workers involved in the cleanup of the damaged reactor, which took more than a decade and cost $1 billion.

since the accident at Three Mile Island (though several that had been ordered before the accident have since been built and put into operation). In order to address the public's fears and concerns, the Nuclear Regulatory Commission was forced to improve the ways in which nuclear power plants operate.

James B. Edwards

During his 1980 presidential campaign, Ronald Reagan promised to abolish the Department of Energy. Americans should rely on private enterprise—not the government—to

THE DEPARTMENT OF ENERGY AT WORK: THE OFFICE OF CIVILIAN RADIOACTIVE WASTE MANAGEMENT

The Office of Civilian Radioactive Waste Management is a program administered by the Department of Energy. Its job is to develop and manage a nationwide system for disposing of spent nuclear fuel from commercial nuclear reactors and high-level radioactive waste from national defense activities, such as weapons production and the construction of nuclear-powered submarines.

solve its energy problems, Reagan said. Soon after taking office, Reagan selected James B. Edwards, the governor of South Carolina, as the nation's third secretary of energy. As energy secretary, Edwards argued for a more limited government role in setting energy policy. Edwards believed that free enterprise could solve most energy problems. Since many of the United States' natural energy resources—its reserves of coal, oil, and natural gas—were controlled by the government, the best thing the government could do to help reduce America's dependence on foreign oil would be to give American companies easy access to these resources. Despite the recent Three Mile Island accident, Edwards also wanted to encourage the further development of nuclear energy by making it easier for companies to get licenses to open and operate nuclear energy plants.

Reagan and Edwards lifted all remaining price controls for gasoline, propane (often used to heat homes), and crude oil. As expected, prices rose, which made some people unhappy, especially those who lived in areas of the country where winters are harsh. However, the high prices made powerful energy companies happy, and their campaign money had helped get Reagan elected. Higher prices also encouraged exploration for crude oil, because new domestic oil reserves would help increase supply and lower prices. In the meantime, Reagan and Edwards pushed plans to let private companies develop the energy resources under government control (such as much of the country's coal and oil sale). In line with Reagan's campaign promise, Edwards hoped to be able to dismantle the Department of Energy as a cabinet-level department. He planned to fold it into another cabinet-level agency, such as the Department of Commerce, but Congress did not allow it.

James D. Watkins

Soon after George H. W. Bush was elected president in 1988, he picked James D. Watkins, a former chief of naval operations for the U.S. Navy with training as a nuclear engineer, to be his secretary of energy. Watkins, a conservative Republican, agreed with Bush that it was best to let the free market determine prices for

An American Black Hawk helicopter hovers above a burning Kuwaiti oil well. In the final days of the Gulf War of 1991, Iraqi dictator Saddam Hussein's invasion of Kuwait was being turned back by an international coalition of troops led by the United States. Hussein ordered his retreating forces to sabotage Kuwaiti oil wells on their way out. More than 700 wells were set on fire. The damage took more than two years and $50 billion to repair.

energy, especially for coal, oil, and natural gas. Watkins was a strong supporter of nuclear energy, but he was also worried about the problem of what to do with the radioactive waste that was a by-product of nuclear energy production.

Two important events related to energy policy and use occurred during Watkins's tenure as secretary of energy. The first of these was the 1990 to 1991 Gulf War, which followed Iraqi president Saddam Hussein's invasion of Kuwait, a small neighboring country in August 1990. Hussein hoped to gain control of Kuwait's valuable oil fields. With the agreement of the United Nations, the United States and a multinational armed force drove Saddam Hussein out of Kuwait. Meanwhile, Secretary Watkins announced plans to increase oil production and decrease consumption to counteract the expected temporary loss of Iraqi and Kuwaiti oil. Oil production was not seriously interrupted, however, and oil prices remained relatively low throughout the 1990s.

A second energy-related crisis that occurred early in George H. W. Bush's presidency was the 1989 *Exxon Valdez* oil spill. The *Exxon Valdez* was a giant oil tanker that carried crude oil from a pipeline in Alaska. It ran aground soon after it had picked up its cargo. Almost 11 million gallons (41,640 kiloliters) of oil spilled into Prince William Sound, creating a slick that covered 1,000 square miles (2,590 sq kilometers). Scientists believe that 40 percent of the 11 million gallons was eventually washed up on beaches, 35 percent of it evaporated, and 25 percent entered the Gulf of Alaska and either washed ashore or was carried out to sea. Some 1,300 miles (2,092 km) of shoreline within Prince William Sound had been oiled, 200 miles (322 km) of that heavily so.

Animals of hundreds of species were killed in the *Exxon Valdez* oil spill. Twenty-three species had their populations reduced enough to make it doubtful they would return to their former numbers. About 250,000 seabirds were killed, along with 2,800 sea otters, 1,000 cormorants, and hundreds of loons, harbor seals, and bald eagles. Of the twenty-three species affected by the spill, only the bald eagle and the river otter have recovered to their pre-1989 population levels.

In the wake of the *Exxon Valdez* accident, the U.S. Congress passed the Oil Pollution Act in 1990. This new law ordered

A worker uses a high-pressure hose to remove oil from the Prince William Sound shoreline following the *Exxon Valdez* disaster in 1989. Today, beaches that had lost plant and animal life due to the toxic effects of oil and the intense cleanup efforts show signs of bouncing back. Yet some beaches are still polluted by oil deposits, and some rocky sites that were stripped of heavy plant cover by high-pressure, hot water cleaning remain mostly bare rock.

changes to be made that would help prevent future oil spills and reduce damage to the environment when spills occurred. Public attention was once more drawn to the difficulty of reconciling energy use with protection of the environment. After the accident, many Americans began to view the oil industry as a profit-obsessed, irresponsible enemy of the environment.

President Bill Clinton's Secretaries of Energy

During his successful presidential campaign in 1992, Democratic candidate Bill Clinton said the Bush and Reagan administrations' energy policies had been too influenced by the big oil companies. He promised to break their hold on energy policy and instead emphasize conservation and fuel efficiency.

Clinton and his vice president, Al Gore, were both strong supporters of pro-environment energy regulation. They promised to develop energy policies that would promote the use of renewable resources (like wind and solar power that cannot be used up like fossil fuels). Clinton's three secretaries of energy—Hazel O'Leary (1993–1997), Federico Pena (1997–1998), and Bill Richardson (1998–2001)—worked to carry out these policies.

The pro-environment aims of Clinton's secretaries of energy were frustrated by one important trend, however. Oil was abundant and relatively cheap throughout the 1990s. Despite the Clinton administration's attempts to encourage conservation, most Americans did not feel that the nation was in the midst of an energy crisis. The compact, fuel-efficient cars of the late 1970s and 1980s gave way to giant, gas-guzzling sport-utility vehicles (SUVs). As the decade wore on, the Department of Energy began to focus less attention on domestic conservation measures and more attention on the disposal of nuclear waste and bomb-making material in the countries of the former Soviet Union.

George W. Bush's Energy Secretaries

George W. Bush (the son of George H. W. Bush) became president in 2001. He and his vice president, Richard Cheney, were both former oil company executives. During his presidential campaign, Bush criticized the Clinton administration's pro-environment energy policies. Bush argued that the development of America's oil reserves was vitally important to the creation of a more abundant supply of energy and decreased American dependence on foreign oil at a time of great political instability in the oil-rich Middle East.

As promised during Bush's campaign, his secretary of energy, Spencer Abraham, pursued policies intended to loosen the environmental regulations that had prevented some of the nation's most delicate and beautiful public lands from being made available for oil drilling and logging. At the beginning of Bush's second term, in January 2005, he appointed Samuel Bodman to the position of energy secretary. Bodman served Bush previously as both deputy commerce secretary and deputy treasury secretary. Though Bodman had little experience with energy policy, as deputy commerce secretary he was responsible for pushing Bush's controversial energy bill through the House of Representatives in 2003, a bill that contained provisions for opening Alaska's Arctic National Wildlife Refuge to oil drilling (which the Senate voted in favor of in March 2005). The bill stalled in the Senate and debate was halted till after the 2004 presidential election. As secretary of energy, Bodman was expected to focus on renewing the push for passage of Bush's energy bill and developing domestic energy supplies. Under President Bush, the energy policy pendulum again swung back toward pro-industry policies and away from environmental protection.

CHAPTER THREE

How the Department of Energy Works

T he basic job of the secretary of energy is to advise the president on energy policy and guarantee that the United States has enough energy to meet its present and future needs. Because energy is crucial to so much of American private and public life and its varied activities—from watching television and cooking dinner to using a computer at school and attending a nighttime baseball game—the activities of the Department of Energy must also be extremely varied.

The department must concern itself with matters as different as ensuring that electric companies charge their customers a fair price to seeing to it that radioactivity from nuclear waste does not leak into groundwater and endanger

Barrels containing nuclear waste are being stored at a facility in Oak Ridge, Tennessee, known as the Y-12 National Security Complex. Y-12 was created in 1943 in order to process uranium—a radioactive element—for use in the first atomic bomb. Today, the facility oversees the dismantling of nuclear weapons, the storage of nuclear materials, and the maintenance of nuclear stockpiles.

the health of nearby residents. The leadership of the Department of Energy is responsible for the operation of a $25 billion organization, which employs more than 115,000 people in thirty-five states. Making sure that America's energy needs are met safely and at a reasonable cost is a very big and very complicated task.

DOE Research

The Department of Energy concerns itself with a wide assortment of problems. Some of them have no obvious relationship to the nation's energy needs. For example, the Department of Energy oversees the research and manufacture of nuclear weapons and the storage of nuclear waste materials. As much as two-thirds of the DOE's almost $25 billion annual budget is spent on matters related to nuclear security or defense.

In addition, the Department of Energy supports many kinds of research projects. Supporting the research and development of alternative energy technologies—such as harnessing solar energy or using hydrogen and oxygen to fuel cars—is hard to argue against, unless you are a member of the oil industry. On the other hand, research into new areas like nanotechnology (the science of microscopic machines) may seem like an odd way for the DOE to spend taxpayer money. Yet one day nanotechnology research may produce results that will revolutionize energy production by, for example, creating far more efficient lightbulbs and increasing the storage capacity of our nation's electrical grid. The results of research are unpredictable. It is not always possible to know which project will produce results that will help to meet the country's energy needs.

The DOE's Four Mission Areas

There are so many different agencies within the Department of Energy that it would take a much longer book than this to describe all of them. However, the DOE's activities can be boiled down to four mission areas that the department is responsible for—energy resources, national security, environmental quality, and science and technology.

Energy Resources

The Department of Energy must see to it that there is enough energy—whether in the form of oil, gas, coal, nuclear, water,

THE DEPARTMENT OF ENERGY AT WORK: THE OFFICE OF SCIENCE

The Office of Science manages DOE research programs in basic energy sciences, biological and environmental sciences, and computer science. The Office of Science is the federal government's largest single funder of research related to materials and chemicals. It also supports U.S. research in climate change, geophysics, genomics (the study of genetics), life sciences, and science education.

wind, or solar energy—to meet the country's needs. This is the DOE's most basic and important duty. Through the Federal Energy Regulatory Commission (FERC), the Department of Energy regulates the sale of energy to businesses and homes. It works to keep electricity prices fair, licenses hydro-electric dams (which convert the energy of rushing water into electricity), regulates the transportation of petroleum products, and grants permission to the companies that want to operate interstate natural gas facilities. A group of DOE agencies—the four Power Marketing Administrations (PMAs)—sells power produced at government-owned hydroelectric dams. The Energy Information Administration (EIA) collects statistics about energy in the United States and around the world. The EIA analyzes the information it collects to make predictions about the country's future energy needs and how they might be met.

National Security

Through the National Nuclear Security Administration (NNSA), the Department of Energy regulates and keeps track of the nuclear energy generated for both peacetime and military uses. It develops nuclear weapons, keeps them in working order, and ensures their safekeeping. The idea of a terrorist or a criminal getting control of a nuclear weapon has provided a premise for many spy novels and blockbuster summer movies. The work of the NNSA helps to keep this nightmare scenario in the realm of fiction where it belongs.

The NNSA is also responsible for providing the U.S. Navy with nuclear engines for its submarines and aircraft carriers. In addition, the NNSA encourages nuclear nonproliferation. "Nonproliferation" means not letting something spread or grow. Nuclear nonproliferation activities involve working to see that countries that do not yet have nuclear weapons do not develop or obtain them and that countries that do have them do not sell them to non-nuclear countries, groups, or individuals. The greater the number of countries that have nuclear weapons, the greater the danger that there will be a deadly nuclear attack or accident. For this reason, nuclear nonproliferation is seen as one of the most important policy goals for any U.S. administration and the Department of Energy.

Environmental Quality

The 1970s, the decade when Americans began to worry seriously about their energy supply, was also the decade when they became more concerned about the environment. In response to growing public concern about air and water pollution, the Environmental Protection Agency (EPA) was established in 1970 by President Richard M. Nixon. It is no coincidence that energy and the environment came to the forefront of national consciousness at the same time.

All forms of energy production and consumption have major effects on the environment. The burning of coal, oil, and gas adds to air pollution. Mining coal can wreck the landscape. Oil spills kill ocean and shore wildlife. Generating nuclear power creates cancer-causing nuclear waste products that can end up in our streams, air, and soil and that can remain poisonous for thousands of years. Even hydroelectric dams and windmills cause some harm to wildlife. Solar power has hardly any negative effects on the environment, but at the moment it is very expensive to produce compared with other ways of generating electricity.

Since the production, distribution, and consumption of energy all have powerful effects on the environment, environmental quality is a major concern of the Department of Energy. One of the DOE's most important environment-related duties is the cleaning up of former nuclear weapons sites, which is handled by the office of Environmental Management.

At the 22nd World Gas Conference in Tokyo, Japan, held in June 2003, a curious conference participant examines Toyota's Fuel Cell Hybrid Vehicle (FCHV). Fuel-cell hybrids are cars that use electricity rather than fossil fuels for power. The electricity is generated by the interaction of hydrogen and oxygen and creates no pollution.

Science and Technology

The Department of Energy employs or funds government scientists and private (nongovernment) scientists to undertake its research projects. Some of this research is aimed at developing new ways of generating and distributing energy, such as research into solar energy and the development of hydrogen-powered electric cars. Other projects the DOE supports have nothing to do with the nation's energy needs but draw on technologies that were originally developed by the nuclear energy industry. For example, the Department of Energy has a medical sciences division, which does basic research in scientific fields such as nuclear medicine. Nuclear medicine uses very small amounts of radioactive materials to diagnose and treat disease. Nuclear medicine can be used to perform stress tests on the heart, scan bones to identify injuries, and scan lungs for blood clots, among other things.

The Department of Energy in the Twenty-first Century

Confronting present challenges and anticipating those of the future are what the secretary of energy's job is all about. The DOE was created during the energy crisis of the 1970s, a time of difficulty that inspired a great concern for the future. Americans had become alert to the fact that their energy supply could not be taken for granted and was not unlimited. People became aware that every major decision the country made about energy policy would lead the country down a different path, toward a different future. The questions being asked at the dawn of the twenty-first century about America's future energy supply are not much different from those asked in the 1970s.

Should the United States continue to use more energy than it can produce within its shores? If the answer is yes, the future might mean being politically blackmailed by the countries that produce most of the world's oil.

Should the United States try to get more oil out of its own land? Drilling at home might result in the destruction of America's wilderness areas, without necessarily ending America's dependence on foreign oil.

Should the United States keep energy costs low by permitting coal-burning power plants to operate without installing expensive equipment that reduces the amount of poisons the plants release into the atmosphere? If so, the United States could look forward to dirtier air and water and more pollution-related illnesses, along with its lower energy bills.

Since oil and coal are nonrenewable resources (all the earth's coal and oil will be used up one day), should we build more nuclear power plants? Nuclear power is both a cheap and renewable resource. Yet a future that includes nuclear power may also include an endless buildup of nuclear waste and occasional nuclear disasters like the 1986 explosion at the Chernobyl nuclear plant in the former Soviet Union. This accident killed thirty-one people immediately and could lead to thousands of radiation-related cancer deaths in the following years.

43

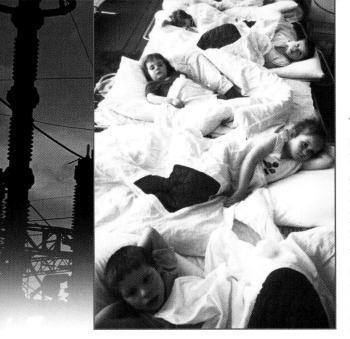

The 1986 explosion of the Chernobyl nuclear plant in the former Soviet Union resulted in thirty-one deaths directly related to the accident. It is thought that several thousands of people exposed to high levels of radiation following the accident will eventually die of radiation-related diseases. These children from a village near Chernobyl are suffering from radiation-related intestinal problems.

 Many scientists believe that the gases emitted by the burning of fossil fuels are contributing to a greenhouse effect, which will lead to a dramatic and possibly catastrophic warming of the earth's surface and change in its climate during the twenty-first century. Should the United States participate in treaties aimed at reducing the world's total production of these greenhouse gases even though it will mean higher prices for both energy and manufactured goods?

 Since the use of energy has so many negative environmental consequences, should the United States encourage its citizens to reduce their use of energy by taxing gas, fuel oil, and electricity? Though this might help the environment, energy taxes might harm the U.S. economy, at least in the short term. It might also make the politicians who support it very unpopular with the voters.

Developing an energy policy that tackles these questions and tries to answer them with concrete actions will almost certainly favor either industry or the environment. Striking a balance between the needs of both will be extremely difficult. As a result, industry will either have to adapt to more strict environmental regulations while the economy slows down during the adjustment or the health and safety of our environment will be sacrificed for the profit of large companies. Whichever direction the DOE chooses, it will anger almost as many Americans as it pleases, and the consequences of its energy policy will have a profound impact on the way we live in the twenty-first century.

The DOE Looks to the Future

Three particular energy problems and proposed solutions that are currently being debated give an idea of the problems that will be faced by future secretaries of energy.

Nuclear Waste Disposal: The Yucca Mountain Nuclear Waste Repository

In 2002, after years of fierce debate among environmentalists, Native American nations, Republicans, and Democrats, the U.S. Congress voted to give final approval to the construction of a nuclear waste repository (storage facility) deep inside a mountain in the Nevada desert. The site, officially known as the Yucca Mountain Nuclear Waste Repository, is located

THE DEPARTMENT OF ENERGY AT WORK: ENVIRONMENTAL MANAGEMENT

The DOE's Environmental Management (EM) program is responsible for cleaning up the soil and water at and around its former nuclear weapons sites. EM cleans up soil using a variety of methods. Sometimes it removes the contaminated soil and stores it in a special facility designed to hold contaminants. Other contaminants can be removed at the site, leaving the soil in place. Occasionally, natural remedies can be used to clean up a site, such as the planting of certain kinds of vegetation that can soak up contaminants.

To clean up contaminated surface water and groundwater, the EM can simply pump the water out of the ground, remove the contaminant, and pump the water back into the ground. Cleaned-up land and water sites are then monitored by the EM for years to ensure that no further contamination occurs.

1,000 feet (305 meters) below Yucca Mountain, about 90 miles (145 km) from the city of Las Vegas. It is scheduled to open in 2010. At that time, it will begin to receive shipments of radioactive nuclear waste from 103 nuclear reactors around the country. Up to 77,000 tons (69,853 metric tons) of this material, which will remain radioactive for hundreds of thousands of years, are expected to be shipped to Yucca Mountain over the next quarter of a century.

Nuclear waste is produced by the power plants that generate nuclear energy and also by the manufacture of nuclear weapons. When human beings are exposed to nuclear waste in large quantities, they get radiation poisoning and usually die quickly. When they are exposed to smaller quantities of radiation, they suffer an increased risk of cancer and birth defects. There is no way to turn nuclear waste into something harmless. Its radioactivity cannot be removed and destroyed. Instead, it must break down on its own over thousands of years. Radioactive materials can only be contained during this long period, and this is not easy to do. Needless to say, nobody wants to live near this material. Burying the material 1,000 feet (305 m) below Yucca Mountain is one way to try to place the dangerous material far from human settlements.

However, there are many questions about the safety of the Yucca Mountain repository. Some say that over time radioactive material stored in the earth will seep into groundwater and then enter nearby rivers, streams, and lakes, eventually finding its way to large population centers. Others point to the danger posed by regularly scheduled deliveries of nuclear waste to a single site in Nevada. What if terrorists learn the delivery schedule and hijack a truck containing nuclear waste? If they get ahold of this material, they could use it to produce a simple and crude bomb that, if exploded, would spread nuclear material over a large area.

Though it looks as though the Yucca Mountain repository will be built, the arguments over it are unlikely to end. Given

A worker walks down half a mile (0.8 km) inside Yucca Mountain in Nevada, where the DOE plans to create a nuclear waste storage facility. The waste would be shipped to the mountain in casks that are heavily shielded to contain the radioactive waste and strong enough to survive crashes, punctures, and exposure to fire and water.

the amount of nuclear waste the United States produces each year, there will be the need for more repositories like the one at Yucca Mountain. The problems of nuclear waste disposal and storage will continue to be a troubling issue for future secretaries of energy.

Nonpolluting Fuels: The FreedomCAR Program

In his January 28, 2003, State of the Union address, President George W. Bush proposed a $1.2 billion research project with the aim of developing clean, hydrogen-powered automobiles.

The president noted that a relatively simple chemical reaction between hydrogen and oxygen can generate enough energy to power cars. These hydrogen-powered cars would not contribute to air pollution because the only waste they would produce is water, not exhaust fumes.

This form of energy discussed by President Bush does seem to have an exciting future. Oxygen and hydrogen are currently being combined to generate electricity in the form of fuel cells. Cars may one day contain fuel cells instead of gas tanks. Many obstacles lie in the path of this invention, however.

One of these obstacles is so basic that it is unlikely that fuel cells will ever be the main solution to either the United States' energy needs or to its air pollution problem. The chief obstacle is that in the case of hydrogen fuel cells, it takes energy to make energy. In fact, a lot more energy is spent obtaining the hydrogen for fuel cells than is actually made by those cells when hydrogen and oxygen are combined to generate electricity.

Hydrogen is the most common element in the universe, but here on Earth it is not available in its free form, uncombined with other elements. We cannot mine it like coal or drill for it like oil or natural gas. It exists mainly in chemical compounds such as water, which is a combination of hydrogen and oxygen atoms. Separating the hydrogen from other elements uses energy, making hydrogen impractical as a major source of power for the nation's energy needs. Some experts feel that fuel cells, or "hydrogen power," will be developed for use as a new kind of battery. It will power some of our gadgets but may never meet our energy needs in any large-scale way or reduce our dependence on fossil fuels.

The DOE will have to figure out the proper role for fuel cells in supplying the nation's future energy needs. At the same time, it will have to continue to explore other clean and renewable sources of energy that can provide the bulk of the power required by Americans.

The Safety of Russian Nuclear Materials

The arms race between the former Soviet Union and the United States, which lasted from the late 1940s to the late 1980s, was a central part of the Cold War. The Cold War was a decades-long, nonmilitary conflict between the two superpowers. The source of this simmering tension was the nations' political differences. The United States promoted democracy and capitalism. The Soviet Union supported a brand of Communism that tightly controlled political and personal freedoms and the economy. While opposing each other, both countries tried to gain influence with the other nations of the world. During the Cold War, each side built enough nuclear bombs to destroy all life on this planet many times over. The two nuclear superpowers faced each other like two gunslingers in the Wild West, their hands ready to draw their weapons with terrible consequences for all.

Then, in the late 1980s, the Communist dictatorship that had dominated Eastern Europe and the Soviet Union collapsed.

A Ukrainian army officer examines a destroyed missile silo near the town of Pervomaisk in the Ukraine, once a republic of the Soviet Union. In 2001, the Ukraine destroyed the last of its missile silos as part of an effort funded by the United States to dismantle and destroy the newly independent nation's Soviet-era nuclear arsenal.

Several regions that had been part of the Soviet Union, such as Lithuania, broke away and became independent countries. The bulk of the former Soviet Union became Russia and began the slow and difficult process of shedding a Communist system in favor of capitalism, democracy, and freedom of speech. The new, weaker Russia was no longer hostile to the United States and was eager to sign treaties with its former enemy that would reduce the number of nuclear weapons in both countries. The world no longer seemed to be always standing on the brink of nuclear war.

One huge problem remained, though: what about the thousands of nuclear bombs and missiles throughout Russia and the newly independent former Soviet republics still armed and pointed at American targets? The bombs and bomb-making materials Soviet scientists created during the arms race are still in Russia. They are guarded by soldiers, many of whom are angry and suffering because they are underpaid, underfed, and poorly housed. The old Soviet Union was a police state that kept everything, including its nuclear facilities, under tight control. The new Russia is perhaps not as closely regulated. What would happen if agents of terrorist networks offered some unhappy, low-level Russian official a few million dollars to secretly hand over one or more bombs that might never be missed? If one of these stolen bombs—or the nuclear material in it—was exploded, the resulting disaster could make the terrorist attacks of September 11, 2001, look small.

To deal with this new nuclear threat to American interests, in the 1990s the DOE developed programs meant to help Russia track and dispose of its nuclear weapons, convert the Russian nuclear weapons program to peaceful uses, and find civilian (nonmilitary) employment within Russia for its nuclear scientists. Otherwise these unemployed or underpaid Russian scientists might be tempted to go to work for countries that are interested in obtaining nuclear weapons. The danger posed by the often unsecured and poorly guarded nuclear materials spread throughout the former Soviet Union will haunt the secretaries of energy for many years to come.

Conclusion

T he secretary of energy has to make tough choices that affect many people. Each decision can lead to different, unpredictable outcomes for America's economy; for people's jobs and properties; for the health of wildlife and the safety of our air, food, and water; and for the long-term future of the world climate. No wonder the activities of the Department of Energy tend to be surrounded by controversy. Every action the secretary of energy takes sparks angry protest from some segment of the population. Lobbyists (paid representatives) for various interests—such as the oil industry or environmental groups—are constantly at work trying to steer energy policy in one direction or another.

A few interested groups of people watch every move made by the secretary of energy. Unfortunately, the rest of us tend to pay much less attention to the DOE's activities and decisions, taking notice only when the lights go out or when there are gas lines around the block. When the immediate problems go away, we tend to forget about our energy supply and its future. That is a mistake. Everything we have learned in the past thirty years about energy, the environment, and world politics should tell us that energy decisions are critical to the future of the whole country and the world beyond our shores. If we want a future that we can all live with, we should all participate in these decisions and think about the kind of world we want our children and grandchildren to inherit.

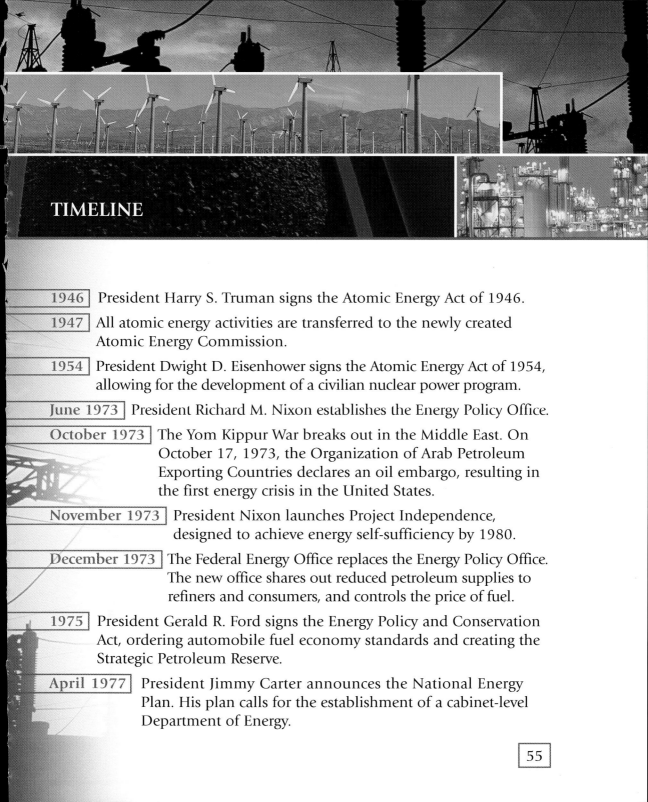

TIMELINE

| 1946 | President Harry S. Truman signs the Atomic Energy Act of 1946. |

1947 All atomic energy activities are transferred to the newly created Atomic Energy Commission.

1954 President Dwight D. Eisenhower signs the Atomic Energy Act of 1954, allowing for the development of a civilian nuclear power program.

June 1973 President Richard M. Nixon establishes the Energy Policy Office.

October 1973 The Yom Kippur War breaks out in the Middle East. On October 17, 1973, the Organization of Arab Petroleum Exporting Countries declares an oil embargo, resulting in the first energy crisis in the United States.

November 1973 President Nixon launches Project Independence, designed to achieve energy self-sufficiency by 1980.

December 1973 The Federal Energy Office replaces the Energy Policy Office. The new office shares out reduced petroleum supplies to refiners and consumers, and controls the price of fuel.

1975 President Gerald R. Ford signs the Energy Policy and Conservation Act, ordering automobile fuel economy standards and creating the Strategic Petroleum Reserve.

April 1977 President Jimmy Carter announces the National Energy Plan. His plan calls for the establishment of a cabinet-level Department of Energy.

August 6, 1977–August 23, 1979 | **James R. Schlesinger**

August 1977 | President Carter signs the Department of Energy Organization Act. James R. Schlesinger is sworn in as the nation's first secretary of energy.

January 1979 | The Shah Mohammed Reza Pahlavi flees Iran. The loss of Iranian oil exports results in a worldwide shortage of oil. Oil-consuming nations are using 2 million barrels of oil per day more than are being produced.

March 1979 | An accident occurs at the Three Mile Island nuclear power plant in Pennsylvania, and a core meltdown is narrowly averted.

June 1979 | President Carter announces increased funds for solar energy research and development.

July 1979 | President Carter proclaims a national energy supply shortage and orders temperature restrictions in nonresidential buildings to conserve oil.

August 24, 1979–January 20, 1981 | **Charles W. Duncan Jr.**

January 23, 1981–November 5, 1982 | **James B. Edwards**

February 1981 | Secretary Edwards announces a major reorganization of the DOE to improve management and increase emphasis on research, development, and production.

May 1982 | As promised in his campaign, President Ronald Reagan proposes legislation transferring most responsibilities of the DOE to the Department of Commerce. Congress declines to consider the legislation.

November 5, 1982–February 7, 1985 | **Donald Paul Hodel**

February 7, 1985–January 20, 1989 | **John S. Herrington**

March 1, 1989–January 20, 1993 | **James D. Watkins**

| 1990 | Iraq invades and seizes Kuwait. Secretary Watkins announces plans to boost oil production and cut consumption to counter Iraqi-Kuwaiti oil losses. |

| January 22, 1993–January 20, 1997 | **Hazel R. O'Leary** |

| October 1993 | President Bill Clinton and Vice President Al Gore introduce the Climate Change Action Plan, emphasizing voluntary measures to control and reduce greenhouse gas emissions. |

| March 12, 1997–June 30, 1998 | **Federico F. Pena** |

| August 18, 1998–January 20, 2001 | **Bill Richardson** |

| September 1998 | Secretary Richardson and Russian minister of atomic energy Yevgeny Adamov sign two agreements designed to help transform Russia's nuclear arms program to peaceful uses. |

| 1999 | The Department of Energy announces the Wind Powering America initiative, designed to greatly increase the use of wind power in the United States over the next decade. |

| 2000 | The department creates the National Nuclear Security Administration (NNSA). The NNSA's mission includes maintaining a safe nuclear weapons stockpile and encouraging nonproliferation. |

| January 20, 2001–January 31, 2005 | **Spencer Abraham** |

| January 2001 | President George W. Bush establishes the Energy Policy Development Group, a task force to be chaired by Vice President Richard Cheney. Members of the group include Secretary Abraham, other cabinet and senior policy officials, and representatives of the energy industry. The meetings are held behind closed doors and their deliberations are kept secret. Critics charge that energy industry officials have been allowed to dictate policy to the administration. No environmental groups are included in the task force. |

May 2001	President Bush releases the National Energy Policy (NEP) developed by his energy task force. The NEP urges actions to meet five specific national goals: modernizing conservation, modernizing the energy infrastructure, increasing energy supplies, accelerating the protection and improvement of the environment, and increasing the nation's energy security.
December 2001	Senate Democrats propose an alternative energy bill that promotes conservation, efficiency, and development of new resources over expanded drilling on public land.
2002	The Senate votes down an amendment to the energy bill that would allow drilling for oil and gas in Alaska's Arctic National Wildlife Refuge.
November 2003	The House of Representatives approves President George W. Bush's energy bill that includes billions of dollars in tax breaks for the oil, gas, nuclear power, and car industries. The Senate blocks the measure, and efforts to pass an energy bill are put on hold until after the 2004 presidential election.
February 1, 2005	**Samuel W. Bodman**
March 16, 2005	The U.S. Senate votes in favor of opening the Arctic National Wildlife Refuge in Alaska to oil drilling.
2010	Nuclear waste will begin to be stored at the Yucca Mountain repository if the DOE's application for a license to operate the storage facility is accepted by the Nuclear Regulatory Commission.

GLOSSARY

cartel A group of commercial producers who join forces in order to limit competition or to set prices at a certain level.

conservation The planned management of a natural resource to prevent its destruction or neglect.

domestically produced oil Oil produced within the borders of one's own nation.

embargo A cutting-off of trade.

global warming A consistent and substantial rise in the average surface temperature on Earth.

greenhouse effect A process in which Earth's atmosphere is warmed due to the interaction of solar radiation and atmospheric gases that are released by the burning of fossil fuels.

greenhouse gases Gases like carbon dioxide and methane that promote the greenhouse effect and global warming.

hydroelectric Relating to the production of electricity by water.

oil reserves Sources of oil on U.S. government property, set aside for future use during energy supply emergencies.

Organization of Petroleum Exporting Countries (OPEC) A cartel of major oil-exporting countries established in 1960 to control the pricing and production of oil. In 2002, more than 77 percent of the world's proven oil reserves lay under the soil of OPEC member nations.

Alternative Energy Institute
P.O. Box 7074
Tahoe City, CA 96145
Web site: http://www.altenergy.org

**American Museum of Science
and Energy**
300 South Tulane Avenue
Oak Ridge, TN 37830
Web site: http://www.amse.org

Nuclear Energy Institute
1776 I Street NW, Suite 400
Washington, DC 20006-3708
Web site: http://www.nei.org

Office of Fossil Energy
U.S. Department of Energy
Forrestal Building
1000 Independence Avenue SW
Washington, DC 20585
Web site: http://www.fe.doe.gov

Sierra Club National Headquarters
85 Second Street, Second Floor
San Francisco, CA 94105
Web site: http://www.sierraclub.
  org/energy

U.S. Department of Energy
1000 Independence Avenue SW
Washington, DC 20585
Web site: http://www.energy.gov

WEB SITES

Due to the changing nature of
Internet links, the Rosen Publishing
Group, Inc., has developed an
online list of Web sites related to
the subject of this book. This site
is updated regularly. Please use this
link to access the list:

http://www.rosenlinks.com/tyg/ener

Ball, Jacqueline A., ed. *Nuclear Energy*. Milwaukee, WI: Gareth Stevens, 2003.

Bickerstaff, Linda. *Oil Power of the Future: New Ways of Turning Petroleum into Energy*. New York, NY: The Rosen Publishing Group, Inc., 2003.

Chandler, Gary, and Kevin Graham. *Alternative Energy Sources*. New York, NY: Twenty-first Century Books, 1996.

Gutnik, Martin J., and Natalie Browne-Gutnik. *The Energy Question: Thinking About Tomorrow*. Berkeley Heights, NJ: Enslow Publishers, Inc., 1999.

Hayhurst, Chris. *Hydrogen Power of the Future: New Ways of Turning Fuel Cells into Energy*. New York, NY: The Rosen Publishing Group, Inc., 2003.

Horn, Geoffrey M. *The Cabinet and Federal Agencies*. New York, NY: Gareth Stevens, 2003.

Jones, Susan. *Solar Power of the Future: New Ways of Turning Sunlight into Energy*. New York, NY: The Rosen Publishing Group, Inc., 2003.

Scarborough, Kate. *Nuclear Waste* (Our Planet in Peril). Mankato, MN: Bridgestone Books, 2002.

Snedden, Robert. *Energy from Fossil Fuels*. Barrington, IL: Heinemann Library, 2001.

Tesar, Jenny E. *Global Warming*. New York, NY: Facts on File, Inc., 1991.

Wellman, Sam. *The Cabinet*. Broomall, PA: Chelsea House Publishers, 2001.

BIBLIOGRAPHY

Crawford, Leslie. *Energy Conservation*. Parsippany, NJ: Dale Seymour Publications, 1997.

"Feds Push Fuel Cells." NewsMax.com. January 10, 2002. Retrieved October 2003 (http://www.newsmax.com/archives/articles/2002/1/9/144451.shtml).

Geller, Howard. *Energy Revolution: Policies for a Sustainable Future*. Washington, DC: Island Press, 2002.

Heinberg, Richard. *The Party's Over: Oil, War, and the Fate of Industrial Societies*. Gabriola Island, British Columbia, Canada: New Society, 2003.

Hoffmann, Peter. *Tomorrow's Energy: Hydrogen, Fuel Cells, and the Prospects for a Cleaner Planet*. Cambridge, MA: MIT Press, 2002.

U.S. Department of Energy. "Institutional Origins of the U.S. Department of Energy." 2002. Retrieved October 2003 (http://www.dpi.anl.gov/dpi2/instorig/insotrig1.htm).

U.S. Department of Energy. "U.S. Department of Energy: 25th Anniversary." 2002. Retrieved October 2003 (http://www.25yearsofenergy.gov).

Wald, Matthew L. "Doubt Cast on Prime Site as Nuclear Waste Dump." *New York Times*. June 20, 1997. Retrieved October 2003 (http://www.state.nv.us/nucwaste/yucca/nys01.htm).

INDEX

A

air pollution, 21, 40, 49
alternative energy sources, 20, 25, 37
Arab oil embargo, 16–19
Arctic National Wildlife Refuge, 10, 34
atomic bomb, 13–14
Atomic Energy Commission (AEC),
    14–15, 23

C

Carter, Jimmy, 11, 19, 21, 23, 24, 25–26
Clinton, Bill, 33, 34
coal, 5, 13, 21, 29, 30, 37, 38, 40, 43, 49
conservation, 10, 20, 21, 24–26, 32–33

D

Department of Energy
    responsibilities of, 23, 35–41

E

Edwards, James B., 28–29
energy crisis, 11–12, 15–16, 19–20, 21, 23,
    25, 31, 33, 42
Energy Information Administration (EIA),
    38–39
energy policy, 9, 11, 15, 19, 20, 24–25, 26,
    27, 28, 30, 32–34, 35, 42, 45, 53
Environmental Protection Agency (EPA), 40
Exxon Valdez oil spill, 31–32

F

Federal Energy Regulatory Commission
    (FERC), 38
fossil fuels, 10, 13, 33, 44, 50

G

gas crisis, 8, 17–19, 25
gasoline, 11, 13, 19–20, 24, 29
greenhouse effect, 44
Gulf War, 30

H

hydroelectric dams, 38, 40

M

Middle East, 11, 13, 15, 16, 34

N

nanotechnology, 37
National Nuclear Security Administration
    (NNSA), 39
natural gas, 5, 29, 30, 38, 40, 49
nonrenewable resources, 43
nuclear power, 5, 10, 13–15, 19–20, 21, 24,
    26–29, 30, 37, 39, 40, 41, 43, 47
Nuclear Regulatory Commission, 27
nuclear waste, 28, 33, 35–36, 40, 43, 45, 46,
    47, 48
nuclear weapons, 14, 36, 39, 47, 51–52

O
oil, 5, 10, 11, 13, 15–19, 20, 21,
    23–25, 29, 30, 31, 32, 33, 34,
    37, 40, 43, 49
Organization of Arab Petroleum
    Exporting Companies (OAPEC),
    16–18, 19
Organization of Petroleum Exporting
    Countries (OPEC), 16–17, 19

R
radioactive waste, 21, 28, 30, 35, 46, 47

T
Three Mile Island accident, 24, 26–28

W
water pollution, 40
waterpower, 5, 10, 12, 37
weapons, 13–14, 17
wind power, 5, 10, 33, 37, 38

Y
Yucca Mountain Nuclear Waste Repository,
    45–48

ABOUT THE AUTHOR

Phillip Margulies is a writer who lives in New York City. He has written numerous books for the Rosen Publishing Group on science, technology, and American history. He is particularly interested in political science and public policy.

PHOTO CREDITS

Front cover (top and portraits), pp. 9 (right), 36 Department of Energy Photo; front cover (bottom), back cover, pp. 4–5, 6–7 (top), 9 (left) © Digital Vision; p. 4 (circle) © Neil Beer/Photodisk/Getty; pp. 6–7 (bottom) © Don Farrall/Photodisc/Getty; p. 12 Library of Congress Prints and Photographs Division; p. 14 © PhotoDisc; pp. 17, 25 © Bettmann/Corbis; p. 18 © Owen Franken/Corbis; p. 27 © Pennsylvania State University Engineering Library; p. 30 © Peter Turnley/Corbis; p. 32 © Exxon Valdez Oil Spill Trustee Council/NOAA; p. 41 © Toshifumi Kitamura/AFP/Getty Images; p. 44 © AP/Wide World Photos; p. 48 © Dan Lamont/Corbis; p. 51 © Reuters NewMedia Inc./Corbis.

Designer: Evelyn Horovicz